1%

This item was
purchased with monies
provided from the
optional 1% sales tax.

D0478381

GAMES FOR ALL YEAR

100 Games for WINTER

BARRON'S

Original title of the book in Spanish: *Juegos para todo el año: Juegos para el invierno*

© Copyright Parramón Ediciones, S.A. 1999—World Rights
Published by Parramón Ediciones, S.A., Barcelona, Spain.
Author: Josep Maria Allué
Illustrators: Maria Puig Pons, Maria Espluga Solé, and Núria Colom Canals

© Copyright of the English language translation 2001 by
Barron's Educational Series, Inc.

All inquiries should be addressed to:
Barron's Educational Series, Inc.
250 Wireless Boulevard
Hauppauge, New York 11788
http://www.barronseduc.com

International Standard Book No.: 0-7641-1757-2
Library of Congress Catalog Card No.: 00-064157

Library of Congress Cataloging-in-Publication Data
Allué, J. M. (Josep Maria)
    [Juegos para todo el año. English]
    Games for all year / J.M. Allue.
      p. cm.
    Contents: [1] Games for summer.
    Includes bibliographical references and index.
    ISBN 0-7641-1754-8 (v. 1)
    1. Games. I. Title.
GV1201.A54 2001
790.1—dc21   00-064157

Printed in Spain
987654321

Contents

To Parents and Educators

Game playing is an innate activity and part of human nature. Its importance in our physical and intellectual development contributes to making game playing an essential part of childhood and to sustaining our interest in games throughout our lives. The spontaneity, pleasure, and joy involved in playing games helps children establish interpersonal relationships and have fun with family, friends, and classmates, regardless of the age or gender of the players.

When we talk about games, we usually refer to a series of activities that are carried out freely for the sole purpose of having fun. While it is true that our desire to play is inborn, what we play depends on the resources available at the moment, such as space, number of players, materials, and familiarity with specific games.

In this respect, games can be orchestrated and, knowing their importance in the physical and intellectual development of young children, resources must be made available for offering children a variety of new and appealing games that encourage them to explore, have fun, and interact with others and their surroundings.

Playing means fun and entertainment. In *Games for Winter* we offer **100** different games whose only requirement from you is a desire to play them!

Games for Winter

The cold temperatures during most of the winter make it difficult for children to play in their usual play areas. Afternoons in the park or weekend outings are less frequent in winter than at any other time of the year.

During the winter, games are often played at home with family and a few friends, making games that require little space and fewer players those most often played. Time-honored, popular games such as board games and games of wit play an important role during the cold weather.

Despite the limitations on playing outside, there are wonderful opportunities for children to play outdoors. Recess and a snowfall in areas where it usually snows are two such opportunities in which children can play games where they run, jump, and release all of their pent-up energy.

The games in this book are divided into five sections. Each game begins with information about the target age range, the recommended time it takes to play each game, the approximate number of players, the materials needed, and the level of activity involved in each game. Following are the sections included in *Games for Winter*:

- **Games of Wit:** There are many games that can be played at home that use the imagination and test skills of observation and drama. Playing these kinds of games allows children to have fun without having to go outside.

- **Table Games:** These are among the oldest kinds of games played. Board games, card games, and games using dice have been played for centuries, always with the same purpose: to entertain and bring us together and to test our intelligence and ability to strategize.

- **Games for the Playground:** Recess in the schoolyard offers children one of the few opportunities to engage in activities that involve movement and speed. The only requirements for playing games such as these are available space and playmates.

- **Party Games:** Birthday parties provide excellent opportunities for children to have fun with friends. Because large groups of friends do not come together so often in winter, parties are especially important and should be filled with games.

- **Games for the Snow:** Snow is wonderful for playing in and provides unlimited possibilities. Children can make forms from snow and can easily romp around in it. Snow is the basis for many games that can be played only during the winter and only where snow is frequent.

Games for All Year

The collection *Games for All Year* compiles **400** games divided into four volumes, one for each season of the year: *Spring, Summer, Fall,* and *Winter.* Each volume presents **100** games selected on the basis of the play area appropriate for individual seasons. The games have been grouped this way to make it easier to select a particular game and to get it started quickly. However, all of the games can be played at any time of the year as long as you have the desire to play them and the time to do so.

J. M. Allué

Games

1

# of Wit

Time spent at home, on a car trip, or on a stroll can be much more fun when it is filled with games. The only requirements for having fun with the games in this section are a quick mind and attention to detail. These games require very little space and materials.

25 games of wit chosen especially to be played indoors. These games will entertain and amuse children, and, at the same time, will enhance their powers of observation and ability to reason and laugh. This is a valuable resource for having fun at home.

Serious Circle

Players test their powers of self-control as they try to keep a straight face while being tickled.

- **Age:** 4 years and up
- **Approximate Time:** 5 minutes
- **Players:** 5 or more
- **Materials:** none
- **Activity Level:** low

1. All of the players stand around in a circle. One player is chosen to begin the game.

2. The first player turns to the player on her right and uses her fingertips to tickle him under the chin, under the arm, and wherever else she decides.

3. During the five seconds she is tickling the other player, she says out loud "Tickle, tickle, tickle." Neither player is allowed to laugh at any time.

4. If both succeed in not laughing, the second player repeats the procedure with the next player. When the game has gone around the entire circle, the second player starts the new round.

There Are Four

In this game, players try to guess how many fingers other players will extend when it's their turn to play.

- **Age:** 5 years and up
- **Approximate Time:** 5 minutes
- **Players:** 2 or more
- **Materials:** none
- **Activity Level:** low

1. Players stand in front of each other or, if there are more than two, they stand in a circle. They decide on an order of play and put one hand behind their back.

2. The first player says "There aaaarrre . . . three!" for example. Then everyone shows their hand with as many fingers extended as they wish.

3. The player counts the total number of fingers extended by the players to see if she guessed correctly. If so, she wins the game; if not, the game continues.

4. The game can be played up to a certain number of guesses. It can be used to decide who will go first in the next game.

Simon Says

This is a well-known game in which the players have to be quick to obey Simon's orders.

- **Age:** 5 years and up
- **Approximate Time:** 5 minutes
- **Players:** 3 or more
- **Materials:** none
- **Activity Level:** low

1. Players stand in a circle around the leader of the game, who takes the part of "Simon." If the players are very young, it is best for an adult to be the leader.

2. Simon gives orders for all of the players to follow. He does so using the phrase "Simon says . . . thumbs up," for example. All of the participants put their thumbs up in the air.

3. When Simon gives an order that is not preceded by "Simon says . . . ," players should not obey that order; rather, they should stay in their places as if nothing had been said.

4. Little by little, Simon picks up the pace of the actions in order to make them harder to do. Players who follow an order they shouldn't or who do not complete an order correctly are out of the game.

4 Who Are You?

A simple game of deduction in which young players have to try to guess the job selected by another player.

- **Age:** 6 years and up
- **Approximate Time:** 10 minutes
- **Players:** 3 or more
- **Materials:** none
- **Activity Level:** low

1. Straws are drawn to choose the player who will start the game. The first player has about 15 seconds to think of the job she will select.

2. Once she has selected a job, she will say "Ready." The other players will take turns asking her questions that require a yes or no answer and try to figure out what the job is.

3. Questions should be like these: "Do you work with food?" or "Do you sell something?" After every three questions, a player can request a demonstration of the job, which the player will act out.

4. If a player thinks he has guessed the job, he can say, for example, "You're a painter." If he has guessed correctly, he must think of a new job for other players to guess. If he guesses incorrectly, he is out of the game.

5 How Many?

A popular numbers guessing game from Tanzania in which players try to win all the beans.

- **Age:** 6 years and up
- **Approximate Time:** 5 minutes
- **Players:** 2 or more
- **Materials:** 15 to 20 beans per player
- **Activity Level:** low

1. Each player receives between 15 and 20 beans or some other object of the same size. Everyone should have the same amount.

2. Players establish an order of play. The first to go puts as many beans as he wants into his hands and puts the others aside so the other players cannot see them.

3. Once the number of beans is chosen, the player extends his closed fist with the beans inside and says "How many?" The rest of the players will say how many beans they think he has hidden in his hand.

4. If a player guesses the exact number of beans, she wins all of the beans that her companion had in his hand. If the player is wrong, she has to give the other player one of her own beans. Then it's the next player's turn to hide the beans.

5. The game is played until one of the players has won all of the beans in the game or until the allotted time for the game is up. In this case, the player with the most beans wins.

6 The Storytellers

Players take turns building on a phrase in a game that stimulates the imagination and makes everyone laugh.

- **Age:** 7 years and up
- **Approximate Time:** 10 minutes
- **Players:** 2 or more
- **Materials:** paper and pencil
- **Activity Level:** low

1. The players sit around a table and each receives a piece of paper and a pencil. Then an order of play is established for giving directions for the game.

2. The first player starts the game by saying a word the others must write about, for example, "Animal," and everyone writes the name of an animal at the top of his or her paper.

3. After players write down the name of an animal, they fold their papers over so that no one else can see what they've written. They then pass their paper to the next player. The second player will say "Did," for example, and everyone writes down an action.

4. Players continue folding their papers over to cover what they've written and continue to add new words, such as "a boy . . . ," "a girl . . . ," "there . . . ," "they see . . . ," "she says . . . ".

5. After the papers have been passed to all of the players and come back to their original owners, they are unfolded and each player reads the short story that resulted.

7 Badum

A game of coordination in which players have to be able to synchronize two movements while trying not to laugh.

- **Age:** 7 years and up
- **Approximate Time:** 5 minutes
- **Players:** 2 or more
- **Materials:** none
- **Activity Level:** low

1. Players stand in a circle so that they can all see each other well. After they are in place, they put one open hand over their belly and the other over their head.

2. Everyone counts together: "One, two, three . . . Go! When they shout "Go," they move the hand they have over their belly in circles and, at the same time, they move the hand over their head up and down.

3. Players continue these movements in unison for as long as they can. While they are doing this, they say out loud very seriously: "Badum, Badum, Badum . . .".

4. Players who laugh or lose the rhythm of the movements cannot start again. The last one left is the winner. This fun game is much more difficult than it seems!

8 Who's Who?

A game of deduction that can be played in newly formed groups so that the participants can get to know each other.

- **Age:** 7 years and up
- **Approximate Time:** 10 minutes
- **Players:** 10 or more
- **Materials:** none
- **Activity Level:** low

1. Players draw straws to select two players who will be "It." These two leave the room or turn their backs to the others while the rest choose a secret player they will try to describe.

2. Once the secret player is chosen, the two players who are "It" come back to the group. The two "Its" then take turns asking the others questions to try to guess which player was selected.

3. The questions must refer to the physical appearance of the players and can only be answered with a yes or no. "Does he wear glasses?" or "Does he have short hair?" are acceptable questions. Players cannot ask whether the selected player is a boy or a girl.

4. "It" can tell those players who do not meet the characteristics they are asking about to sit down. After each question, there will be fewer players left standing.

5. After a question, one "It" can say who he thinks the secret player is. If he is right, he is the winner; if he is wrong, he loses a turn and the other "It" can ask two questions in a row.

9 This Way

A game of expression in which players try to interpret the meaning of an adverb by applying it to a concrete action.

- **Age:** 8 years and up
- **Approximate Time:** 10 minutes
- **Players:** 3 or more
- **Materials:** none
- **Activity Level:** low

1. Players draw straws to see who will start the game. The player who starts should think of an adverb that ends in "ly," such as happily, rapidly, foolishly, and so on.

2. Once the adverb is chosen, the other players will have to try to guess what it is. In order to do so, they will ask the player to act out some actions that are related to the chosen adverb. The player will perform the actions so that all of the others can see.

3. The players can ask her to run this way, to sing this way, to laugh this way, or whatever other action comes to mind.

4. Each player can ask her to act out only one action and that player then has only one opportunity to guess what adverb the player is trying to describe. The one who wins will think of and act out the next adverb.

10 Initials

A vocabulary game in which the initials of players' first and last names tell them how to answer the questions.

- **Age:** 8 years and up
- **Approximate Time:** 10 minutes
- **Players:** 4 or more
- **Materials:** none
- **Activity Level:** low

1. Players get into a circle and establish an order of play to see who will ask the first question and what the order of play will be for the rest of the game.

2. The first player asks the player to his right a question such as "What are your favorite things to eat?"

3. The player has to respond with two words that begin with the initials of her name. For example, if her name is Martha Williams, she might say, "Macaroni and watermelon."

4. Each player answers the question when it is his turn. A player who answers incorrectly or takes more than five seconds to answer is eliminated.

5. When everyone has had a turn to answer the question, the second player thinks of another question for others to answer.

11 Scrambled Syllables

A vocabulary game requiring a good memory to remember which syllables have already been said.

- **Age:** 8 years and up
- **Approximate Time:** 5 minutes
- **Players:** 3 or more
- **Materials:** none
- **Activity Level:** low

1. Players establish an order of play. The first player will start the game by saying any syllable, for example, "por."

2. Each of the following players will say the first syllable that comes to his mind, such as: "ta," "da," "ble," "so," etc. If only a few players are playing, they can go around more than once.

3. Players will try to memorize the syllables offered; when there are five or more, they will take 30 seconds to try to mentally combine them, trying to form the longest word possible.

4. When time is up, each player will say the longest word he came up with, in this case, "soda," "table," or "portable." Whoever comes up with the longest word wins a point.

12 Animal, Vegetable, or Mineral?

A very entertaining game of deduction in which players try to guess what their companion is thinking by asking him questions.

- **Age:** 8 years and up
- **TApproximate Time:** 5 minutes
- **Players:** 2 or more
- **Materials:** none
- **Activity Level:** low

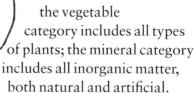

1. Players draw straws to select a player who will think of something for the others to guess. She lets the other players know when she has chosen something, and they ask "Animal, vegetable, or mineral?"

2. The animal category includes all living things except vegetables; the vegetable category includes all types of plants; the mineral category includes all inorganic matter, both natural and artificial.

3. After the first question is answered, players can ask as many other questions as they wish. The only answers can be "yes," "no," or "I don't know."

4. Players can try to guess after each set of three questions they ask. They can have as many tries as possible. The first player to guess correctly will think of the next object.

Hands and Feet

A game of coordination in which players should know the names of body parts well so that they do not make a mistake during the game.

- **Age:** 8 years and up
- **Approximate Time:** 5 minutes
- **Players:** 6 or more
- **Materials:** none
- **Activity Level:** average

1. A game leader is chosen who will stand up while the rest of the players sit in a circle on the floor. Each player sits with his feet behind the player to his right.

2. The game leader will call aloud the parts of the body players should touch and how they should touch them. For example, "Behind, left hand, right foot" would mean that players should touch the right foot of the player behind them with their left hand.

3. All of the players will follow the commands as fast as they can. The game leader will slowly pick up the pace of the game, making the orders to be followed a little more difficult.

4. Players who make mistakes can be eliminated from the game, or the game can be played simply for fun with no one being eliminated. Every now and then, the game leader should be changed.

14 Forbidden Letter

A vocabulary game in which everyone tries to answer their playmates' questions without saying the forbidden letter.

- **Age:** 9 years and up
- **Approximate Time:** 5 minutes
- **Players:** 2 or more
- **Materials:** none
- **Activity Level:** low

1. Players draw straws to determine who will choose the forbidden letter. Whoever is picked will say a letter and that letter cannot be said from that moment on—nor can any word that has that letter be said.

2. Once the letter is determined, players have to ask each other random questions and do so very carefully so they do not use any word that includes the forbidden letter.

3. Players try to confuse each other into using the forbidden letter. If the forbidden letter is S, a player could ask, "Where did the *Titanic* go down?" in order to force one of them to say "In the sea."

4. Players who use the forbidden letter are out of the game. The last one to remain is the winner. If after a while no one makes a mistake, more than one forbidden letter can be used.

15 The Pile

A fun game in which players have to recognize the voices of their friends to avoid having them sit on their backs.

- **Age:** 9 years and up
- **Approximate Time:** 5 minutes
- **Players:** 5 or more
- **Materials:** none
- **Activity Level:** low

1. Players draw straws or play a simple game to choose "It." The player chosen lies face down on the floor.

2. Then, so that "It" doesn't know who the player is, players use signs to tell another player to sit on him. "It" then asks this player to imitate an animal in an effort to recognize him.

3. If "It" recognizes who is sitting on him, that player has to take his place lying on the floor. Otherwise, the player "It" mistakenly names is added to the pile.

4. Players continue adding to the pile until "It" identifies the player who sat on him first. Everyone has to be very careful in this game, and if at any time "It" says "I give up," all of the players have to immediately get off of him.

True or False?

Players ask questions to find out which of their companions' statements are true and which are purely fiction.

- **Age:** 10 years and up
- **Approximate Time:** 10 minutes
- **Players:** 3 or more
- **Materials:** none
- **Activity Level:** low

1. Players draw straws to see who will start the game. The player who starts will make three statements about himself, such as, "My brother is a taxi driver," "We have three dogs at home," and "Yesterday I went to the movies."

2. One of the three statements has to be true and the other two have to be false. Each player will ask three questions to guess which one is true.

3. When all of the players have asked their questions, each can then say which statement he or she believes is true. The players who get it right receive a point.

4. The player who made the three statements gets one point for each player he fooled with his statements. The game is played until a predetermined score is reached, depending on the number of players.

Buzz

A game of mental agility in which simple counting becomes a difficult task requiring a great deal of attention.

- **Age:** 10 years and up
- **Approximate Time:** 5 minutes
- **Players:** 5 or more
- **Materials:** none
- **Activity Level:** low

1. Players establish an order of play in which the first player starts again after the last player has taken a turn. Once this is done, players choose a number to buzz, for example, 3.

2. Everyone agrees to substitute this number with an onomatopoeic sound, such as "buzz." From then on, each time a number contains a 3, it will be substituted with a "buzz."

3. The first player starts the count and play moves to the right. Each player will count off a number, but 13 will be said as "1-buzz," 30, "buzz-zero," and 33, "buzz-buzz."

4. Players who make a mistake are out of the game and the chosen number changes. The game can be made more challenging by playing with more than one "buzzed" number or by having the multiples of the chosen number "buzzed" as well.

The Detective

A game of observation in which the player who is the detective tries to identify the assassin before others are eliminated.

- **Age:** 10 years and up
- **Approximate Time:** 30 minutes
- **Players:** 10 or more
- **Materials:** paper and pencil
- **Activity Level:** low

1. Players sit in a circle facing each other. One of the players cuts out as many small pieces of paper as there are players and draws an X on one of them and an O on another.

2. This player then gives a piece of paper to each player. The player who gets the paper marked with an X is the assassin; the one who gets the paper with an O is the detective who will try to catch him.

3. The assassin can kill any other player he wishes by winking at him. He can also make another player an accomplice by sticking his tongue out at him. When the assassin kills someone, the player he kills calls out "Dead." Accomplices can wink in order to kill but cannot stick their tongues out to make new accomplices.

4. The detective cannot be killed. If the assassin tries to do so, he is caught. When the detective sees someone winking his eye, he calls this out. If the person who winked is the assassin, the detective wins. If the person who winked is an accomplice, he says so and the game continues.

19 The Three Investigators

A game of deduction involving a difficult challenge, since the chosen object has to be uncovered by asking very few questions.

- **Age:** 10 years and up
- **Approximate Time:** 10 minutes
- **Players:** 8 or more
- **Materials:** an object in the room
- **Activity Level:** low

1. Players decide among themselves or draw straws to choose three players to be investigators. These players leave the room and the rest choose an object that the investigators will try to discover.

2. Once the object is chosen, the players call the investigators so that they can try to figure out what it is. Each investigator can ask only three questions and can name only one object.

3. The investigators can agree among themselves which questions each will ask. Investigators cannot ask a player if he or she is carrying the object, but they can ask if a companion is carrying it.

4. After the questions have been asked, each investigator says what she thinks is the object they are looking for. If they guess right, they win the game and continue being the investigators.

20 "I'm Going to . . ."

A short imaginary trip during which players use the initial letter of their destination in order to pack the appropriate luggage.

- **Age:** 10 years and up
- **Approximate Time:** 5 minutes
- **Players:** 5 or more
- **Materials:** none
- **Activity Level:** low

1. An order of play is established. The first player says "I am going to . . ." and names a country or city that begins with the first letter of the alphabet, for example, "Argentina." Then he names an object to pack, also beginning with an *A*.

2. Players take turns packing by saying, for example, "I'm going to Argentina and I'm packing apples." The second player adds to that by saying, for example, "I'm going to Argentina and I'm packing apples and anchovies."

3. When each player has said something, the second player will name another destination, continuing alphabetically with *B*.

4. Everyone adds objects that begin with the letter *B*. After each complete round, play continues with the next letter of the alphabet until all of the letters have been used.

21 The Mystery Person

In this game the players have to guess the person their teammate is thinking about, knowing only the first letter of the person's name.

- **Age:** 10 years and up
- **Approximate Time:** 10 minutes
- **Players:** 6 or more
- **Materials:** none
- **Activity Level:** low

1. Players draw straws to see who will begin the game. This starting player thinks of a famous person and when she has decided on one, she says the first letter of the person's name.

2. The next player tries to think of a person whose name begins with that letter and asks yes or no questions about the person to try to guess the mystery identity.

3. A player who receives a "yes" answer can continue asking questions until he receives a "no" answer. Then the next person asks a question.

4. If a player guesses the person his teammate was thinking of, that player gets to think of the next mystery person.

22 Zip, Zap, Zup

A game of reflexes in which players move their heads from side to side in order to start a rapidly changing chain of gestures.

- **Age:** 11 years and up
- **Approximate Time:** 5 minutes
- **Players:** 6 or more
- **Materials:** none
- **Activity Level:** low

1. Players sit in a circle facing each other. The first player slowly turns his head to the side and says "Zzzzzzzip!"

2. The player he looks at can repeat the gesture and the sound in the same direction, or he can say "Zip Zap." In this case, when he says "Zip" he moves his head in the same direction, and when he says "Zap" he turns his head quickly to the other direction and repeats the sound to the previous player.

3. A player who receives a sound can also say "Zup" as he looks at someone who is not directly next to him; this player will then pass the sound on.

4. The game gets increasingly faster until it is impossible to keep up the rhythm. Players who make a mistake or who do not respond on time are out of the game.

Three Errors

Players invent a short story in which they include several errors that they hope will not be detected.

Age: 11 years and up
Approximate Time: 30 minutes
Players: 5 or more
Materials: none
Activity Level: low

1. Players establish an order of play. The first will start to tell a story to the rest of the players, which he will make up on the spot.

2. Throughout the story, the player who is narrating will intersperse a fact that contradicts what was previously said, for example, "four of the three little pigs . . ." or "he went up to the basement . . . ."

3. If a player picks up on the error, she says it, and the turn passes to the next player, who will continue the story from the point at which the previous player left off. If nobody picks up on the error, the same player continues the story.

4. When a player succeeds in including three errors in his story without being detected, he tells the rest of the players, counts up the errors, and wins the game.

Headlines

A very amusing game in which players are newspaper editors who make up the most ridiculous and absurd headlines.

Age: 11 years and up
Approximate Time: 30 minutes
Players: 4 or more
Materials: pencil and paper
Activity Level: low

1. Players take turns saying a letter out loud until there are four letters. If there are more players, they will say their letter in the second round.

2. Everyone writes the letters on their piece of paper. Before continuing, everyone takes a minute to create a headline using all of the mentioned letters.

3. The words of the headline should have the mentioned letters as the first letter in each word in the order in which they were written down. If the letters were: P, R, E, and Z, for instance, they could write "Pursuit of a Red Elephant through the Zoo."

4. After each player has read his headline aloud, everyone votes on the funniest one. The player who came up with it receives a point and the game starts again.

Tap, Tap

A game of coordination in which the players have to be very aware of the gestures of the other players in order to respond in the correct way.

- **Age:** 11 years and up
- **Approximate Time:** 10 minutes
- **Players:** 7 or more
- **Materials:** none
- **Activity Level:** low

1. Players sit in a circle on the floor with their knees bent and their feet apart in front of them.

2. Each player will put his right foot in front of the left foot of the player next to him. One of the players will pick up his foot and tap the floor with his heel to start the game.

3. The player whose foot is next to the foot of the player who started the game will repeat the gesture so that it goes around the circle. When a player taps twice instead of once, the direction is reversed.

4. If a player taps the floor with both feet at the same time, it means that now the game will be played with the hands. This same player pats the floor with his hand and the game continues in the same direction that was being played.

5. When someone taps twice, the direction changes, and if a player slaps his knees with his hands, the game is once again played with the feet. When someone makes a mistake, he stops playing with the foot or hand he made the mistake with.

Table

100

Games

Table games have been and are still one of the favorite pastimes of people of all ages all over the world. Throughout the centuries, these types of games have spread from one country to another, expanding and adapting to each arrival point, becoming a common bond among people of all cultures.

30 table games from all over the world, from the simplest and best known to the most complex and unusual. All of them can be made using cardboard, scissors, and markers, and players can enjoy themselves playing in their homes or wherever else they may be.

Old Maid

This is one of the simplest and most amusing games that can be played with a deck of cards. Nobody will want to get stuck with the Old Maid in his hand!

- **Age:** 6 years and up
- **Approximate Time:** 10 minutes
- **Players:** 2 or more
- **Materials:** a deck of Old Maid cards
- **Activity Level:** low

1. Shuffle all of the cards in an Old Maid deck. Deal out all of the cards to the players. With a regular deck of cards, the Queen of Hearts can become the Old Maid after removing the other queens.

2. Each player looks at his cards to make pairs. If he can make a pair (with the same number, if playing with a regular deck), he puts the pair in the middle of the table.

3. Once all the pairs are on the table, the first player picks a card from the player to his left, looks to see if it makes a new pair to set on the table, and offers his hand (without showing the face) so that the next player can take a card.

4. Players continue picking cards and placing pairs on the table. Players who get

rid of all their cards are out of the game until the only card in play is the Old Maid. The player who gets stuck with that card at the end of the game is the Old Maid.

The Farm

In this game, quick reflexes and a good memory are fundamental in order for players for get rid of their cards in a fun way.

- **Age:** 6 years and up
- **Approximate Time:** 10 minutes
- **Players:** 3 or more
- **Materials:** a deck of playing cards
- **Activity Level:** low

1. The deck of cards is dealt out to all of the players. Then each player chooses a different animal and a sound to identify it, such as, "A cat: Meow!" and the player says it to the others.

2. With their cards face down in one hand, players take turns turning up a card,

covering those already shown with the new card.

3. Everyone looks at the cards that are turned up to see if any number is repeated. When this happens, each player whose card matches the one turned up has to make the sound of his opponent's animal before the opponent does.

4. The first player to make the correct animal sound of the other gives her his pile of cards on the table. When a player is out of cards, he leaves the game. Play continues until only one player is left.

Achi

A simple African game of strategy in which players try to line up three of their chips on the same line.

- **Age:** 6 years and up
- **Approximate Time:** 5 minutes
- **Players:** 2
- **Materials:** cardboard, pencil, 4 white chips and 4 black chips
- **Activity Level:** low

1. Draw a board game on the cardboard as shown in the illustration. Players take their chips and decide who will go first.

2. In turn, players will place one of their chips on one of the intersecting lines on the board. Players try to get three chips on the same line at the same time that they try to block their opponent.

3. Once all of the chips are placed on the intersections, each player during his turn will move one of his chips to an adjacent free space, with the same object of lining up three chips on the same line.

4. The player who succeeds in placing three chips in a row on the board is the winner of the game.

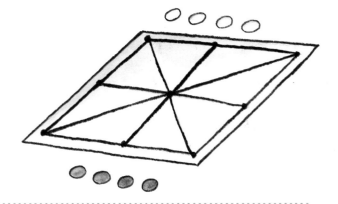

Go-moku

This game of Japanese origin is played all over the world; variations include *Renju* and *Ninuki-Renju*.

- **Age:** 6 years and up
- **Approximate Time:** 5 minutes
- **Players:** 2
- **Materials:** cardboard, marker, ruler, white chips and black chips
- **Activity Level:** low

1. A grid is made like the one shown in the illustration. The squares should be 1 inch on each side and there should be between 13 and 19 rows.

2. The game is started with an empty board. Each player takes a turn to put one chip on the intersection of two lines, trying to get five chips in a row before his opponent does.

3. Once the chip has been placed, it cannot be moved for any reason.

4. The first player to get five chips in a vertical, horizontal, or diagonal line wins the game.

Eight Stacks

In this simple game of strategy, players will try to be the first to have 4 of their cards showing on the board to win the game.

- **Age:** 6 years and up
- **Approximate Time:** 5 minutes
- **Players:** 2
- **Materials:** cardboard, marker, scissors
- **Activity Level:** low

1. Each player makes eight 2-inch-square cards and marks them with a symbol for easy recognition. Then they draw a rectangular board game made up of 2 rows with 4 squares in each.

2. Players take turns placing one of their cards on a square. They can either put their card on an empty square or they can cover another card with it. The object of the game is for players to end up with four of their cards showing on the board.

3. When it is their turn, players can place a new card on a square or they can move a card from one pile to another. However, they cannot look beforehand to see which card will be uncovered if they take one from the top of the pile.

4. The first player to succeed in having four of his cards showing wins the game. The loser will begin the next game, if one is played.

Dominoes

The game of dominoes is said to have been taken to Europe from China, where it originated. These are some simple rules for playing the game.

- **Age:** 6 years and up
- **Approximate Time:** 10 minutes
- **Players:** 2 or more
- **Materials:** a set of dominoes
- **Activity Level:** low

1. Put all of the 28 dominoes face down and mix them up. Each player then takes seven pieces. If more than four people are playing, the pieces are distributed equally and the leftover ones kept for later.

2. Each player looks at her pieces without letting others see them. Whoever has the double six puts it in the center. If nobody has it, the next lowest set of doubles starts.

3. The next player puts a piece with a six touching the double on one side. If a player cannot place a piece, she picks from the leftover pile, if there is one, until she gets a piece she can play.

4. When it is her turn, a player should put down a piece with the same number as those that are at the ends. If it is a double, she must place it sideways. If it is not a double, she continues the line.

5. The first player who manages to get all of her pieces down wins the game.

32 Hyena in Pursuit

A game of tag, very popular in North Africa, in which players try to reach a village without being caught by the hyena.

- **Age:** 6 years and up
- **Approximate Time:** 5 minutes
- **Players:** 2 or more
- **Materials:** cardboard, marker, a die, a different-colored chip for each player
- **Activity Level:** low

1. On a piece of cardboard, draw a circle that will represent a well and another that will represent the village. Draw a path from the village to the well, as shown in the illustration. One player will be the hyena and the other the water carrier, the person who goes to the well.

2. The two playing pieces are put inside the village and the water carrier starts the game by rolling the die three times in a row. For each point, players move into a circle of the path to the well.

3. After the water carrier's three rolls of the die, it's the hyena's turn. From then on the players roll only once per turn. When the water carrier reaches the well, he needs a six in order to leave it. If, on the way back, a player rolls a six, he rolls again.

4. In order to enter the village again and be safe, the water carrier has to roll the exact number. The hyena tries to roll the exact number needed to land in the water carrier's box and eat him before he reaches the village.

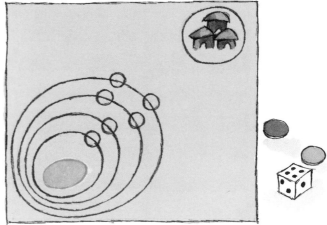

33 Dead!

In this simple but exciting game, everyone tries to get the most points without being eliminated from the game.

- **Age:** 7 years and up
- **Approximate Time:** 5 minutes
- **Players:** 2 or more
- **Materials:** paper, pencil, five dice, a shaker
- **Activity Level:** low

1. Players write their names on a piece of paper and establish an order of play. The first player receives the shaker with the five dice inside and starts the game.

2. Each player takes a turn throwing all of the dice. If the player doesn't roll a two or a five, she records the points she got and rolls again.

3. If a player rolls a two or a five, she doesn't get any points and she eliminates the dice that show one of these numbers and continues to play with the others.

4. When a player loses all of the dice, she says "Dead!" and it's the next player's turn. The player who scores the most points wins.

XO

A game of strategy that takes its name from the symbols players put on their chips (an X or an O).

- **Age:** 7 years and up
- **Approximate Time:** 5 minutes
- **Players:** 2
- **Materials:** cardboard, marker, 5 chips marked with an X, and 5 marked with an O
- **Activity Level:** low

1. On a piece of cardboard, draw a board game consisting of 20 squares arranged in 5 rows and 4 columns. On each side, alternate the placement of the chips.

2. Players draw straws to see which chips will belong to each one and who will be the first to move. Each player sits on the side of the board where his pieces are in the corners.

3. Players take turns moving one of their pieces to an adjacent box. They can move the pieces horizontally, vertically, or by jumping over an adjacent box to a free one.

4. Pieces cannot be moved diagonally and cannot be captured. The first player to succeed in lining up three of his pieces in a row, either horizontally or vertically, wins the game.

35 Donkey

A fun card game in which players try to collect all 4 cards with the same number, say "Donkey" fast, and not lose the hand.

- **Age:** 7 years and up
- **Approximate Time:** 5 minutes
- **Players:** 3 or more
- **Materials:** a deck of cards
- **Activity Level:** low

1. For each player, four cards with the same number are taken out of the deck. Then, these cards are shuffled and dealt out to the players.

2. Each player looks at the cards he has in his hand and decides which number he will collect. Then he chooses one that he does not want, and he gets ready to pass it.

3. Everyone says "One, two, three, donkey!" as they pass the card to their right, putting it face down on the table. Then each player takes the card that has been given to him and sees if he wants it.

4. Players keep on repeating the phrase and passing cards until someone has collected four of the same number. When that happens the player shouts "Donkey," and puts his hand in the middle of the table.

5. Everyone then quickly puts a hand on top. The last player to put his hand on top of the pile receives one letter of the word "Donkey," for example, D. The game continues until someone completes the word and loses.

36 Puluc

A game of Mayan origin that was played with kernels of corn and twigs on the floor of the cabin. This version is an adaptation.

- **Age:** 7 years and up
- **Approximate Time:** 10 minutes
- **Players:** 2
- **Materials:** cardboard, 5 white chips and 5 black chips, 4 two-sided "dice" (coins can also be used)
- **Activity Level:** low

1. Draw a board game with a path of 19 small boxes. This is the "bej," which means path. The "dice" can be kernels of corn with one side marked, or they can be coins.

2. Players take turns rolling the dice twice and moving a chip, with only one chip being allowed in play at a time. One player starts at one end of the board and the other player starts at the other end.

3. A toss that results in dice that have one marked side facing up is worth 1 point; two facing up is worth 2 points; three, 3 points; four, 4 points; no marked side showing is worth 5 points.

4. When a player lands in a box that has her opponent's chip, she captures the chip but does not remove it from the game. Instead, she drags it until she leaves the board at the other end, at which time she eliminates the chip.

5. The pieces that have not been eliminated can be put back into play. Players continue taking turns until one of them loses all of her chips.

The Five Paths

A game from northern China that is usually played with small chocolate candies as game pieces, making eating them an incentive to winning.

- **Age:** 7 years and up
- **Approximate Time:** 5 minutes
- **Players:** 2
- **Materials:** cardboard, marker, 5 black chips and 5 white chips
- **Activity Level:** low

1. Draw a square game board with four rows of four boxes. Put the chips of the same color on the intersections of each of the two opposite sides in order to start the game (1).

2. Players take turns moving one of their chips to an adjoining intersection that is empty, following a straight line. The chips can be moved forward, backward, or sideways.

3. When a player succeeds in lining up two of his chips next to one of his opponent's chips, and if there are no other chips on the same line (2), he can remove his opponent's chip from the board.

4. The game continues until one of the players is left with only one chip. If the game is played with chocolate pieces, players eat the pieces as they capture them.

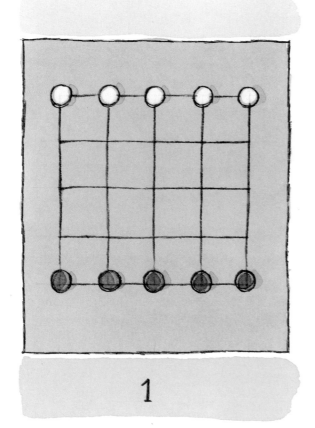

1

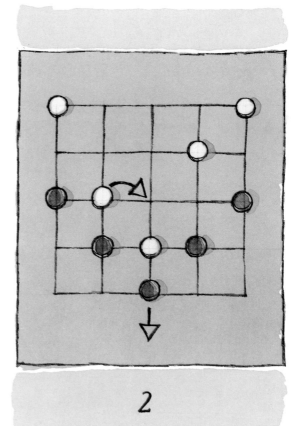

2

38 Zamma

A game played in the Sahara that is related to checkers, as both derive from an Arab game.

- **Age:** 7 years and up
- **Approximate Time:** 10 minutes
- **Players:** 2
- **Materials:** cardboard, marker, 20 white chips and 20 black chips
- **Activity Level:** low

1. Use the marker to draw the game on cardboard, following the illustration. Players place the chips at the starting position and draw straws to see who will get what color and who will begin the game. Each player moves one chip a turn.

2. The chips can be moved only forward or diagonally, but can capture another piece by jumping over it in any direction onto an empty space. If a piece can capture another piece and fails to do so, it is taken out of the game.

3. When a piece crosses the entire board and reaches the last line at the other side, it becomes a "king" and can move as many spaces as it wants to on the same line. It can jump to capture more than one piece, but it cannot change directions to do so.

4. The player who succeeds in eliminating all of his opponent's pieces wins the game. This game can be played with pebbles on sandy ground.

The Series

A dice game in which players must roll the greatest number of repetitions for each one of the numbers.

- **Age:** 7 years and up
- **Approximate Time:** 10 minutes
- **Players:** 2 or more
- **Materials:** paper, pencil, a shaker, 5 dice
- **Activity Level:** low

1. Players make a chart with their names and the numbers of the dice. One player records the scores and fills in the table.

2. The first player throws the dice and decides which number he will play, depending on which one is most often repeated. If he throws three 5s, he sets them aside and throws the rest.

3. Each player throws three times during each turn and at the end counts one point for each dice with the chosen number. If he throws five of the same number, he picks them all up and gets another roll.

4. The results of each player for that number is recorded on the chart. Players cannot play again with the same number, but must choose another number on the next turn. When all of the numbers have been played, points are tallied up to see who the winner is.

		·	·.	·.·	::.	:::
MARÍA	3					
PABLO				4		
IGNACIO		5				
NIEVES					2	

Turkish Checkers

Checkers is a popular game that has an infinite number of rule variations, depending on the country where it is played.

- **Age:** 7 years and up
- **Approximate Time:** 10 minutes
- **Players:** 2
- **Materials:** a checkerboard, 16 white chips and 16 black chips
- **Activity Level:** low

1. All of the chips are placed on the board as shown in the illustration and each player chooses a color. A chip is moved with each turn.

2. Chips can be moved vertically and horizontally, forward and backward. An opponent's chip can be captured by jumping over it into an empty space.

3. If possible, a player can make a chain of jumps to capture more than one of the opponent's pieces. If a chip reaches the last line on the board, it becomes a king.

4. A king can move as many spaces as it wants to on the same line. The player who eliminates all of her opponent's pieces wins the game.

41 Four Alike

A game in which players have to line up four pieces that have something in common.

- **Age:** 7 years and up
- **Approximate Time:** 10 minutes
- **Players:** 2
- **Materials:** cardboard in 2 colors, paper, marker, scissors
- **Activity Level:** low

1. Draw a game board made up of four rows with four squares in each. Then cut out four squares and four triangles in each color.

2. Mark half of the pieces with an X and start the game. Players take turns placing one of their pieces on a square on the board.

3. Each player tries to line up four pieces that have something in common, which could be shape, color, or the X. The player who places the last piece in the series wins.

4. When a player succeeds in lining up four related pieces, he says "Four alike" and wins the game. If anyone forms a series without realizing it and passes the turn to the next player, that player can say it and claim victory.

....

42 Ati Dada

A game of strategy, of African origin, which can be played indoors on a game board or outside on a board drawn in the sand.

- **Age:** 7 years and up
- **Approximate Time:** 5 minutes
- **Players:** 2
- **Materials:** cardboard, marker, 20 small sticks
- **Activity Level:** low

1. On the cardboard, draw a game board like the one shown in the illustration. Each player then takes 10 sticks to play with. To differentiate the sticks of each player, you can paint some of them or break off an end.

2. Each player takes a turn to put one of her sticks in an intersection of two lines or on the corner of one of the squares, trying to put three sticks on the same line.

3. Each time a player forms a line with three of her sticks, she removes her opponent's sticks from the board. When all of the sticks have been placed on the board, one is moved per turn to a free space on the same line. A stick cannot be moved two times in a row on the same line.

4. The player who leaves her opponent with two sticks is the winner.

43 Tablut

A game that originated in Lapland in which one player controls the Muscovite soldiers and the other controls the Swedish soldiers and king.

- **Age:** 8 years and up
- **Approximate Time:** 30 minutes
- **Players:** 2
- **Materials:** cardboard, marker, ruler, 16 black chips and 9 white chips
- **Activity Level:** low

1. Mark one of the white game pieces to be the king and then place all of the chips on the board as shown in the illustration (1). Chess pieces can also be used.

2. The chips move horizontally or vertically over as many spaces as desired. If a player wants to capture an enemy chip, he must move one of his chips in such a way that the enemy chip lies between two of his own (2). However, if the enemy chip is the one that moves between two opposing pieces, it cannot be captured (3).

3. The king is found in his throne or "konakis," which is the position in the middle that only the king can occupy. The king is captured if he is surrounded by four Muscovites or by three if the free side is the "konakis."

4. If the king reaches the edge of the board, the Swedes win. If the king is captured during the game, the Muscovites win the game.

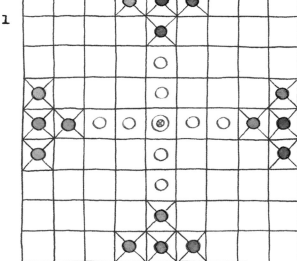

1

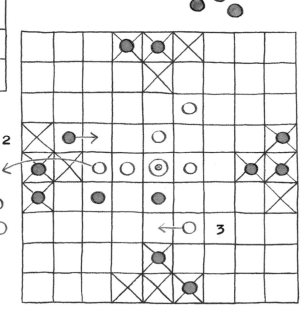

2

3

44 Solitaire

Invented in France in the eighteenth century, this game quickly spread throughout the world. This is the best-known game, which, though difficult, has a solution.

- **Age:** 8 years and up
- **Approximate Time:** 30 minutes
- **Players:** 1
- **Materials:** cardboard, marker, 33 beans
- **Activity Level:** low

1. The original boards were made of wood and the balls of ivory or marble. The game can be made by drawing 33 circles on a piece of cardboard and putting a bean in each one.

2. After the beans have been placed, the one in the center is removed. The object of the game is to eliminate all of the beans, except for one, so that the last bean occupies the center space.

3. To eliminate a bean, the player has to jump one bean over another to an empty space that's behind it. Each jump will be made with a different bean or with the same one that has just been moved. More than one jump can be made.

4. If the jumps are well planned, and if they can be combined, all of the beans can be eliminated, with the last one remaining in the center. It is difficult, but it is possible.

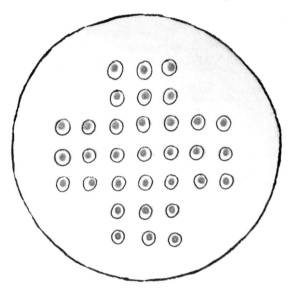

45 Draw Two

A game in which all of the players will pay careful attention to each card that is played so that they don't have to draw. There are many versions to this game.

- **Age:** 8 years and up
- **Approximate Time:** 10 minutes
- **Players:** 2 or more
- **Materials:** a deck of cards
- **Activity Level:** low

1. Deal the cards, giving seven to each player and leaving one in the middle. The remaining cards are put in a pile for players to draw from. The game starts with the player to the right of the dealer.

2. The next player has to throw a card with the same number or the same suit that was thrown before. If she cannot, she loses a turn.

3. If anyone throws a 3, the next player loses her turn and play skips over her; if a 2 is thrown, the next player draws two cards or throws a 2, and two are added to the player to her right. If a 7 is thrown, the direction of the game is reversed.

4. If a player makes a mistake, any of the other players can say "Draw two!" to make that player draw two cards. When a player has only one card left, she has to say "One left!" before any other player orders her to "Draw two!"

5. The first player to get rid of all of her cards wins the game and deals the next round.

46 Seega

A game, which originated in Egypt, whose objective is to capture all of the opponent's pieces. It can also be played on sand.

- **Age:** 8 years and up
- **Approximate Time:** 10 minutes
- **Players:** 2
- **Materials:** cardboard, marker, 12 white and 12 black chips
- **Activity Level:** low

1. A game board is drawn like the one shown in the illustration (1). Players draw straws to see who will place his chips first. Players place two of their chips on each turn.

2. The center space should stay empty at the start of the game. The player who places the last two game pieces will start the game. A game piece may move to an adjacent empty space. Moving diagonally is not permitted.

3. A player captures an opponent's chip by moving in such a way that it remains between two of his own (2). If a capture is possible, it must be done. Each time a player makes a capture, he takes another turn.

4. When a piece is in the center position, it cannot be captured. If all of a player's pieces are blocked, the opponent plays again to open up the board.

5. The player who captures all of his opponent's pieces wins the game.

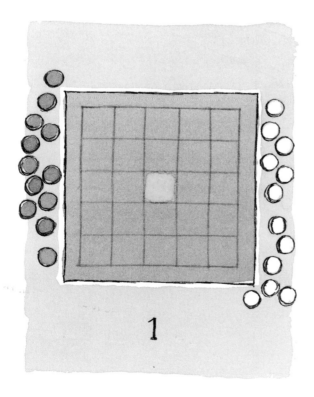

1

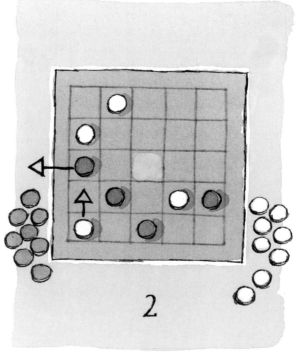

2

47 Awelé

This game of African origin is played all over the world and can be played on a wooden board or with holes dug in the sand.

- **Age:** 8 years and up
- **Approximate Time:** 30 minutes
- **Players:** 2
- **Materials:** 1 egg carton, 48 beans
- **Activity Level:** low

1. Make a game board by putting four beans in each hole of a standard 12-hole egg carton. Each player is assigned the holes on one side.

2. In turn, each player takes all of the beans from one of her holes and, moving counterclockwise, distributes them one by one into the other holes.

3. If the last bean a player distributes ends up in an opponent's hole that contains two or three beans, she takes these. If the hole before the last one also has two or three beans, she takes them, too. The player continues in this way until another number remains or until she gets back to her own holes.

4. If the player distributes beans all around the board, the first hole is left empty. If a player doesn't have any more beans, the other player will move to give her one. If this doesn't work, each player picks up her beans and the game ends. The player who ends up with the most beans wins.

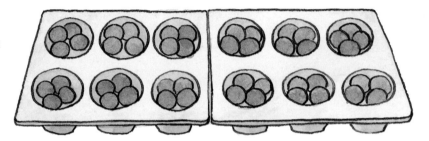

48 Five!

In this game requiring quick reflexes, players have to mentally calculate how many of the same numbers are on the board at any given moment.

- **Age:** 8 years and up
- **Approximate Time:** 10 minutes
- **Players:** 2 or more
- **Materials:** 2 decks of cards
- **Activity Level:** low

1. Separate numbers 1 to 5 from the decks and deal them to players. Players put their cards face down without looking at them. When it is their turn, they turn one up in front of them.

2. When cards of the same suit that add up to five are shown on the board, such as a two of hearts and a three of hearts, everyone says "Five!" and, at the same time, puts a hand in the center of the table.

3. The first player to put his hand down will pick up all of the cards on the table and add them to his pile. If a player makes a mistake and puts his hand down when the cards do not add up to five or add up to more than five, he has to give a card to each of the other players.

4. Players who have no cards left in their hand leave their pile on the table and are out of the game. The player who succeeds in getting all of the cards wins the game.

Thirty-six

Players roll the die and try to get as close as possible to 36 without going over; otherwise, they are out of the game.

- **Age:** 8 years and up
- **Approximate Time:** 5 minutes
- **Players:** 2 or more
- **Materials:** die, a shaker
- **Activity Level:** low

1. Players determine an order of play and draw straws to see who will go first. This player picks up the die and shaker and starts the game.

2. Players can throw the die as many times as they want to on their turn. The number shown on the die with each toss is added to a player's score.

3. The object of the game is to end up with a score that is as close to 36 as possible. To

do this, players can toss as many times as they wish.

4. Players who go over 36 are out of the game. At the end of the game, the player whose score is exactly 36 or closest to that number wins.

Kiriki

In kiriki, players have to surpass the toss of other players or know how to fool them into thinking that they did.

- **Age:** 9 years and up
- **Approximate Time:** 10 minutes
- **Players:** 2 or more
- **Materials:** 2 poker dice, a shaker, paper, and pencil
- **Activity Level:** low

1. The first player throws the dice and looks at them without showing them to the others. Then she covers them with the shaker and says the combined score she got on the dice.

2. Black is worth 1; red, 2; the jack, 3; the queen, 4; the king, 5; and the ace, 6. In addition to the scores, players can also get pairs. The highest score for a pair is with a black and red combination known as "kiriki." The combination of king and ace is known as "a brick."

3. Each player throws the dice and announces a throw higher than the

previous one, whether this is true or not. If the other player believes her, she tosses or picks up the shaker.

4. A player loses when she is caught lying or when she lifts the shaker on a true toss. When this happens, the player adds a letter from the word "kiriki" to her score and the second round begins. The first player to end up with all of the letters of the word loses.

The Hus

This game originated in South Africa where game boards made of stone have been found in several places. It is a distant cousin of the game Awelé (see page 40).

Age: 9 years and up

Approximate Time: 30 minutes

Players: 2

Materials: cardboard, 32 egg carton compartments, glue, 48 beans or small stones

Activity Level: low

1. A game board is made by placing egg carton compartments in 4 rows of 8, and placing the beans inside as shown in the illustration. Players can move the beans only on their side of the board.

2. Players draw straws to see who will go first. This player empties one of his holes and, moving clockwise, distributes the beans one by one into the other holes. If he ends up in an empty hole, he loses a turn.

3. If a player's last bean ends up in a hole that already contains beans, he takes these beans as well and continues distributing them. If the last bean ends up in a hole on the inside row, the player will check to see whether the hole on the inside row of his opponent has beans. If so, he will take these beans as well.

4. If he takes beans from his opponent's inside row, he will check to see if the hole next to the opponent's outside row has beans and takes them, too. If he takes beans from his opponent's outside row, he can empty any hole of his choice in the same row.

5. After he has collected all of the beans, the player distributes them, starting with the last hole where he placed one. When the last bean ends up in an empty hole, play passes to the other player.

6. Players must always begin their moves from a hole that has at least two beans. The game ends when a player succeeds in capturing all of his opponent's beans.

Go

Deeply rooted in Japan and Korea, this game originated in China where it is known by the name "wei qi." The following are the basic rules of the game.

- **Age:** 9 years and up
- **Approximate Time:** 30 minutes
- **Players:** 2
- **Materials:** cardboard, marker, 40 black pieces and 40 white pieces
- **Activity Level:** low

1. The traditional game boards for Go consist of 19 parallel vertical and 19 horizontal intersecting lines. For this game, we will use an easier board made up of 9 lines by 9 lines.

2. Each player will take a turn placing one of her pieces on the intersection of two lines, including margins and corners. A player does not have to place a piece and can pass his turn.

3. Once a piece is placed, it cannot be moved unless it is captured. Go pieces are called stones and play always begins with the black ones. Captured stones are returned to their owner and are taken out of play.

4. A stone is captured when it is surrounded by an opponent's stones. If a stone (1) or a group of stones (2) does not have an adjacent free intersection connected to it by a line, it is removed from the board. A diagonal free space that has no connecting line can still be captured.

5. If to make a capture a player has to put a stone on a point surrounded by enemy rocks (3), when she captures an opponent's stones she creates other free boxes and her stone will remain alive. If only one stone is captured, a player cannot immediately return to capture in this position.

6. The game is played until a player uses up all of her 40 pieces. The winner is the player who at the end of the game dominates most of the board. Each player controls the intersections she occupies with her pieces and the free ones that her stones surround.

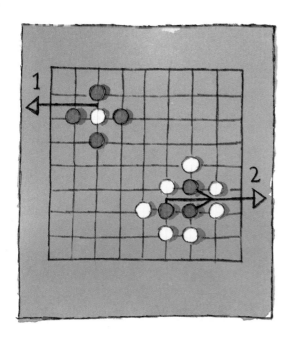

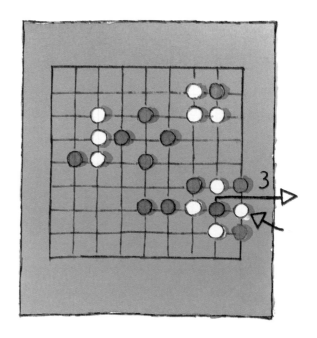

53 Chicago

Players throw the dice to try to get a score one number higher than the number of the round being played.

- **Age:** 9 years and up
- **Approximate Time:** 10 minutes
- **Players:** 2 or more
- **Materials:** 2 dice, a shaker, paper, and pencil
- **Activity Level:** low

1. Players establish an order of play so that the first player begins again after the last player has taken a turn. Then players' names are written on a piece of paper to keep score.

2. In the first round, each player rolls the dice once trying for a 2, in the second a 3, and so on up to 12.

3. If a player rolls one more than the number of the round, he wins those points and it's the next player's turn.

4. At the end of round 11, the player who has scored the most points wins.

54 Crowned!

An exciting game in which players try to win as many points as they can from their opponents.

- **Age:** 10 years and up
- **Approximate Time:** 30 minutes
- **Players:** 2 or more
- **Materials:** 5 poker dice, a shaker, paper, and pencil
- **Activity Level:** low

1. Players establish an order of play and write their names on a score card. The first player to get more than 25 will be crowned the winner.

2. The first player makes up to three tosses and sets aside the dice she wants that will give her the most doubles. All of the players will make the same number of tosses as the first.

3. The order of scoring is: black, red, jack, queen, king, ace. The ace is like the joker. Three reds are worth more than three blacks, but three blacks are worth more than two kings. The more doubles come up in each toss, the more it is worth.

4. One point is played in each round. The player who throws the lowest combination wins the point. If the first player gets four queens, she says as play passes to the next person "four queens are worth one," because this is the lowest toss at this point. The player who throws lower than this wins.

5. If a player rolls five of the same dice, she says "Doubles" and adds another point to the round. If she "doubles" without aces as jokers, she says "Natural" and adds two points instead of one.

6. At the end of each round, the player who makes the lowest throw wins the point. If the round ends in a tie, the points are divided up by rounding them upward.

The King

A card game in which players try to become the king. It is played in different countries under different names.

- **Age:** 10 years and up
- **Approximate Time:** 30 minutes
- **Players:** 3 or more
- **Materials:** 3 decks of cards
- **Activity Level:** low

1. Make a stack of cards to play with by separating from the decks one 1, two 2s, three 3s, and so on until reaching twelve 12s (i.e., kings). Then players draw to see who will be the pawn and who will be the king, depending on who gets the highest card.

2. The king will be first and the pawn last. The pawn deals the cards and clears the table. Then the pawn deals out all of the cards. The king passes his lowest card to the pawn, who, in turn, gives the king whatever card he wants to give him.

3. The king starts the game by putting down all of the cards he wants to of the same number, for example, three 12s (kings). The next player will have to put down three cards of a lower number in order to get rid of cards, like three 10s, and so on, successively.

4. A player can pass if he cannot or does not want to put down any cards. The last player to put down cards starts the next round. The first player to get rid of all of his cards will be the king in the second game. The last player will be the pawn.

Games

100

for the Playground

Playground games are one of the favorite school activities of boys and girls. It is a good idea to have a wide selection of games available for children that will allow them to have fun, stay in shape, and strengthen their friendships.

15 games of movement, races, and tag that children can play with their friends as long as there is large enough space. This can be the schoolyard, the neighborhood, or the park.

56 The Circle

A game that tests the reflexes of young children. An adult leads the game.

- **Age:** 3 years and up
- **Approximate Time:** 5 minutes
- **Players:** 3 or more
- **Materials:** a piece of chalk
- **Activity Level:** average

1. Use the chalk to draw a circle on the floor large enough for players to stand in, with enough space between them so they can move around.

2. Everyone stands with their feet together around the circle. The game leader starts the game by saying "In!" Players respond by jumping inside the circle.

3. The players do the opposite if the leader says "Out!" If the leader say "In," or "Out," and all the players are already there, everyone stays in place.

4. The leader alternates and repeats the two words in such a way that players have to be careful not to make a mistake moving or staying in place.

57 The Ring

A very simple game in which players form a circle that will change based on instructions given by the game leader.

- **Age:** 3 years and up
- **Approximate Time:** 5 minutes
- **Players:** 6 or more
- **Materials:** none
- **Activity Level:** average

1. All of the players hold hands and form a circle. One of the players will be the leader, who does not leave the circle. If the players are very young, it is a good idea for an adult to be the leader.

2. After the circle is formed, the game leader says "The circle is shrinking." Then all of the players walk toward the center, squeezing in to make the circle as tight as possible.

3. Then the leader says "The circle is getting bigger." With that, all of the players move away from each other without letting go of each others' hands.

4. The leader will alternate different orders that players must follow. For example, "The circle bows, jumps, spins . . ." The game can continue until players want to play another game.

Prisoners

In this game, "prisoners" try to escape from the circle formed by the other players, who try to keep them trapped.

- **Age:** 5 years and up
- **Approximate Time:** 10 minutes
- **Players:** 8 or more
- **Materials:** none
- **Activity Level:** average

1. One out of every three players is randomly chosen to be a prisoner. The remaining players will form a circle around them by holding hands and standing feet to feet with the players next to them.

2. The prisoners will gather in the center of the circle and decide on a secret signal for escaping. After they do this, they will walk slowly around the inside of the ring.

3. When one of the prisoners gives the agreed sign, they all try to escape through the openings in the circle. The players who form the circle cannot move their feet, but they can raise and lower their arms or put their knees together.

4. The prisoners cannot grab other players trying to separate them. The players who form the circle count to 10. If the players in the middle of the circle have not been able to escape by the end of the count, the three players return to the middle of the circle and start again.

The Tunnel

A simple, noncompetitive game in which young children will have a lot of fun as they try to get through the tunnel formed by their friends.

- **Age:** 5 years and up
- **Approximate Time:** 5 minutes
- **Players:** 8 or more
- **Materials:** none
- **Activity Level:** average

1. Players get together in pairs. If there is an odd number of players, they look for another one before starting the game. After the children have paired up, they draw straws to see which pair will go first.

2. The children in the first pair stand face to face and put their hands on each other's shoulders, forming an arch with their bodies.

3. The remaining pairs line up in the same way, forming a tunnel. Once they are all in position, the first pair takes each other by the hand and, bending over, pass through the tunnel.

4. When they reach the end of the tunnel, the first pair assumes the tunnel position and says, "Ok!" so that the next couple does the same. The longer the tunnel, the more fun the game is.

60 Trios

A game of tag in which players help each other not get tagged by "It."

- **Age:** 5 years and up
- **Approximate Time:** 10 minutes
- **Players:** 6 or more
- **Materials:** none
- **Activity Level:** high

1. Players draw straws to choose "It." The player who is chosen stays in one place counting to 10 or singing a song so that the other players have time to get away.

2. After she finishes counting, "It" runs to tag her companions. If she succeeds in tagging one, that player becomes "It."

3. If a player is being chased, he can save himself by getting together with two other players. Then the three hold onto each other and say "Trio." "It" cannot tag them then.

4. When players form a trio, "It" moves away to tag another player. Then the trio breaks up. These players will not be able to form another trio until another player becomes "It."

61 Switch Teams

In this game, players have to be very quick and agile in order to trap players from the other team and not be trapped themselves.

- **Age:** 6 years and up
- **Approximate Time:** 10 minutes
- **Players:** 6 or more
- **Materials:** chalk
- **Activity Level:** average

1. Players form two equal teams. Then a line is drawn on the floor with chalk to separate the two sides.

2. Each team gathers on opposite sides of the line. The players on one side try to trap the players on the other side and bring them to their side.

3. When one player captures another, each tries to get the other to cross the line and step on the other side. The player who crosses the line becomes part of the other team.

4. Players can help a teammate bring an opponent across the line; however, they should do so carefully and not use too much force. The game ends when only one player is left on a side.

The Lightbulb

In this game, "It" gives the signal for others to run away, but not before they answer a question.

- **Age:** 6 years and up
- **Approximate Time:** 10 minutes
- **Players:** 5 or more
- **Materials:** chalk
- **Activity Level:** average

1. Players draw straws to choose "It." "It" draws a large lightbulb on the floor and stands on the tip. The other players stand inside the bulb.

2. "It" names a category that everyone has to give a response to. For example, "Names of Flowers." Players then take turns saying the name of a flower and jumping into the bulb.

3. When all of the players are inside the bulb, "It" will say "Lightbulb." Players cannot run out of the bulb until the entire phrase has been said.

4. "It" can try to confuse the others by making a false start or by saying half of the phrase, for example. If a player leaves the bulb prematurely, that player becomes "It." Otherwise, the first player who is tagged becomes "It."

Circle Soccer

This ball game is played inside a circle formed by players. It should be played with a soft ball.

- **Age:** 7 years and up
- **Approximate Time:** 10 minutes
- **Players:** 12 or more
- **Materials:** a soft ball
- **Activity Level:** average

1. A circle is formed with two-thirds of the players. The remaining third stands in the center with the ball. For this game sponge-rubber balls are appropriate because they are heavy without being hard.

2. The players in the center put the ball on the floor and pass it among themselves. They can try to kick the ball out of the circle at any time to score a goal.

3. The players in the circle will try to stop it without using their hands. A goal is valid when the ball leaves the circle close to the floor, below knee level.

4. Each team gets 10 tries to make a goal. After they have taken all of their turns, they count up the goals they made and another team goes into the center. Those leaving the center move into the circle.

64 "ABC"

A name game in which all of the players switch places at the same time, trying not to end up in the middle and be "It."

Age: 7 years and up
Approximate Time: 10 minutes
Players: 7 or more
Materials: chalk
Activity Level: average

1. Players draw straws to choose "It." The others stand in a circle about 6 feet apart around "It." Then with the chalk they draw a circle around their feet.

2. After the circles have been drawn, "It" calls out a letter, for example A. All of the players who have that letter in their name have to run and change places.

3. "It" tries to get into one of the places while the others are switching. The player left without a place becomes "It" and stands in the middle.

4. If "It" says "Alphabet!" all of the players have to change places. The player who is left without a place becomes "It" in the next round.

65 Jump Rope Race

In this race, players try to come in first by jumping in the way that was agreed upon without losing their footing.

Age: 8 years and up
Approximate Time: 5 minutes
Players: 2 or more
Materials: a jump rope for each player
Activity Level: high

1. Each player receives a jump rope before starting the game. A finish line is marked and a goal about 65 feet away. The distance will vary depending on the age of the players.

2. The players get in line and decide how they are going to jump rope to the end: jumping normally, jumping with their feet together, or jumping with one foot at a time.

3. Everyone starts at the same time and advances in the indicated way to the finish. If a player loses his rope or jumps in a different way, he has to start from the beginning.

4. The first player to successfully arrive at the finish wins. If all of the players know how to jump well, there can be more than one race with different styles.

66 Friendly Handkerchief

An amusing variation of the handkerchief game in which laughter and fun are most important.

- **Age:** 8 years and up
- **Approximate Time:** 30 minutes
- **Players:** 11 or more
- **Materials:** a handkerchief, a piece of chalk
- **Activity Level:** high

1. A game leader is chosen to hold the handkerchief and call out the numbers. The other players form two teams and are assigned numbers.

2. Three separate parallel lines are drawn about 7 feet apart. The game leader stands at one end of the middle line holding the handkerchief in her hand.

3. The game leader will then call between one and five numbers. The players who have been assigned those numbers will leave to pick up the handkerchief and take it back to their team.

4. If the game leader says one number, the player will take off running. If he says two numbers, the players go piggyback. If he says three, two of the players will make a seat for the third. If he says four, they will form a throne, and if he says five, they will form a litter to carry the fifth player.

5. The player or players who arrive at their place with the handkerchief will eliminate those who also tried to get it.

67 Flying Ball

This adaptation of volleyball can be played with the sole objective of having fun with friends.

- **Age:** 8 years and up
- **Approximate Time:** 30 minutes
- **Players:** 8 or more
- **Materials:** a ball, a volleyball net
- **Activity Level:** high

1. Players form two teams with the same number of players on each, and mark a 60- by 30-foot rectangular court to divide in half. One player stretches his hand over his head to see how high to put the net.

2. Each team goes on one side and draws for the serve. A player on the team who wins the serve goes to one of the back corners and slaps the ball to the other side.

3. Players on the other team have to return the ball without catching it. They have to return it by slapping it with an open palm or with their fist. The ball is allowed to bounce once when it first comes over the net and a player can touch it three times to return it.

4. If the team who serves fails, the serve passes to the other team; if the other team serves and misses, the first team gains a point and serves again. The game is usually played to 15 points.

68 The Shepherd's Goat

The thief will try to steal the goat from the shepherd without getting caught, but the problem arises when she doesn't know the identity of the shepherd guarding the goat.

- **Age:** 9 years and up
- **Approximate Time:** 10 minutes
- **Players:** 10 or more
- **Materials:** a handkerchief
- **Activity Level:** average

1. Make two knots at two points of a handkerchief to simulate the horns of a goat. Players draw straws to see who will be the thief. This player takes off looking for a hideout; the others form a circle around the goat.

2. Without letting the thief hear, players choose one of them to be the shepherd.

Once this is done, they tell the thief that she can come looking for the goat.

3. The thief will inspect the ring and will separate players' hands so she can enter the circle. The thief grabs the goat and, leaving through the same opening, takes him to his hideout.

4. At the moment the thief touches the goat, the shepherd takes off in pursuit. If he catches the thief, they switch roles. Otherwise, they continue playing the same way. The thief can make a fake attempt to grab the goat to see if the shepherd moves and his identity is revealed.

69 Passes Between Bases

One of the teams will pass the ball with the most precision so that the other team cannot move to catch it.

Age: 9 years and up
Approximate Time: 30 minutes
Players: 10 or more
Materials: a piece of chalk, a ball
Activity Level: average

1. Players split up into two equal teams and draw straws to see who puts the ball into play. Then players move about 40 feet away from each other and draw respective circles around themselves.

2. The players on the second team spread out over the playing field between the two circles. Players on the first team try to pass the ball to their teammates in the other circle, while players on the second team try to intercept it.

3. The players inside the circle cannot leave it and players outside the circle cannot enter it. This means that the passes have to be as precise as possible.

4. The first team scores 2 points for each successful pass. The second team scores 1 point for each interception. The game is played to 10 points; then teams switch roles.

70 Knock Down the Pin

Each team tries to knock down the pin with the ball. To do this, they need to get around the goalie on the opposing team.

Age: 10 years and up
Approximate Time: 30 minutes
Players: 10 or more
Materials: a piece of chalk, a ball, a bowling pin
Activity Level: average

1. Players form two teams, with each one choosing a goalie. Then a playing field is drawn made up of a 70-foot square divided in half. A circle about 15 feet in diameter is drawn in the center.

2. The ball, the pin, and two goalies are placed in the center of the circle. The outside players pass the ball or try to steal it from the other team. Both teams try to knock down the pin with the ball.

3. Each goalie will intercept the throws of the other team to keep the pin from being knocked over. The goalies cannot touch each other.

4. Each time a team knocks down the pin, it scores a point. The team that wins 10 points first wins. After every 2 points scored, the goalies are changed.

party

100

Games

Birthday parties and other kinds of parties are special times that children look forward to with great anticipation. Games are an important and indispensable part of any party, providing the joy that makes a party a huge success.

20 party games that can be played inside the home, guaranteeing that everyone leaves with happy memories of the celebration. When playing these games, emphasis should be placed on fun and camaraderie, regardless of who wins.

71 Treasure Hunt

A treasure hunt is appealing to young children. It's often the first game played at a party.

- **Age:** 4 years and up
- **Approximate Time:** 10 minutes
- **Players:** 6 or more
- **Materials:** crepe paper, party favors (balloons, confetti, streamers)
- **Activity Level:** average

1. Before starting, an adult should wrap up some party favors in colorful paper, making two or three little packages for each player.

2. The packages should be hidden throughout the house where the party will be held. Then all of the participants gather together in one of the rooms.

3. The game leader will ask players to go and look for the packages. When one is found, it should be placed in a common pile without being opened.

4. When all of the packages have been found, players sit down around the pile and take turns opening one of the packages. They keep the contents of the package they open, regardless of who found it.

72 Colorful Hands

In this game all of the participants will have to touch the color named by the leader, but only on the clothes of the other player.

- **Age:** 4 years and up
- **Approximate Time:** 5 minutes
- **Players:** 5 or more
- **Materials:** none
- **Activity Level:** low

1. One of the players will be the game leader. If participants are very young, an adult will take this role. The leader stands up and the rest form a circle around him, leaving a hand's distance between each other.

2. The players take off their shoes and stand in their stocking feet. The leader will then name a foot or a hand and a color, for example, "Right hand, red."

3. Each player will touch with his or her right hand an article of red clothing that the other player is wearing. Players cannot leave their position in the circle, but they can bend over or stretch out their arm.

4. The leader will continue giving new directions such as "Left foot, green," until all of the players lose their balance and the circle breaks up. A new game leader will be chosen for the second game.

Circle of Bubbles

A team game with soap bubbles that will amuse all of the players while at the same time making them move quickly.

- **Age:** 4 years and up
- **Approximate Time:** 10 minutes
- **Players:** 8 or more
- **Materials:** water, soap, wire, plastic cups
- **Activity Level:** average

1. Two teams are formed with an equal number of players on each. One team takes charge of blowing the soap bubbles. To do this, each member of the team receives a cup of water and soap, and a wire wand.

2. The team making the bubbles stands in a circle. Players on the other team are the "bubble hunters" and stand in the center of the circle.

3. At the signal, the bubble makers start to make all the bubbles they can. The bubble hunters try to pop them as fast as possible before they reach the floor.

4. The bubble makers count aloud all of the bubbles that reach the floor. When they reach a predetermined number, the teams switch roles and the game starts over.

Time to Get Dressed!

Each team distributes some old clothes to its members to see who can get dressed the fastest.

- **Age:** 4 years and up
- **Approximate Time:** 10 minutes
- **Players:** 8 or more
- **Materials:** various articles of old clothing
- **Activity Level:** average

1. Players form two teams with the same number on each. If there are a lot of players, more than two teams can be formed. Players line up in single file and the first player on each team receives three articles of clothing.

2. Each team receives the same articles of clothing, which can be a coat, a cap, and two gloves. At the starting signal, the first player on each team puts on the clothing as fast as she can.

3. After players have put their articles of clothing on top of the clothes they are wearing, they

say "Ready!" At that point, the players remove the clothes and pass them to the next player, who repeats the procedure and passes them along to the next person.

4. The first team that succeeds in getting the clothing to their last player to be put on wins the game.

Mystery Taste

A tasting game that will surprise players as they taste foods without seeing them.

- **Age:** 5 years and up
- **Approximate Time:** 10 minutes
- **Players:** 5 or more
- **Materials:** a blindfold for each player, a variety of foods
- **Activity Level:** low

1. The game leader prepares small portions of foods, such as cheese, apple, sugar, and lemon, before starting the game.

2. Once the foods are prepared, players gather around a table and cover their eyes. The game leader then hands out one of the foods, putting it in the hand of each player.

3. When everyone has some, the leader gives the signal for them to taste it. Players put the food in their mouth and then say what they think it is. The sensation is always surprising and many times players do not recognize it.

4. If there are a lot of players, the game can be played with two people at a time, while the others watch. The watchers will have as much fun as the tasters, as they witness the reactions to the food.

76 Stepping on Balloons

A fun activity in which players try to step on everyone else's balloon, while trying to make sure that no one steps on and pops theirs.

- **Age:** 5 years and up
- **Approximate Time:** 5 minutes
- **Players:** 5 or more
- **Materials:** 1 balloon per player, string, scissors
- **Activity Level:** high

1. Each player receives a balloon to start the game. The balloons are inflated and knotted. Each player ties a balloon to his ankle with the string. Once this is done, players move to the wall, leaving the center area free for play.

2. At the signal, all of the players walk to the center of the room trying to pop the others' balloons by stamping on them, while trying to keep others from popping theirs.

3. Players who lose their balloon can no longer try to pop others' balloons and are eliminated from the game. They have to return to the wall while the game continues.

4. The player who succeeds in keeping his balloon intact until the end of the game wins. More than one game is usually played.

5. Because the games are so quick, new balloons are usually given out and another game is played immediately after the first one.

77 Musical Chairs

A variation of the popular game in which players all try to sit on a few chairs.

- **Age:** 5 years and up
- **Approximate Time:** 10 minutes
- **Players:** 6 or more
- **Materials:** 1 chair fewer than the number of players, a radio, tape, or CD player
- **Activity Level:** average

1. All of the chairs are placed in a circle with the backs facing inside. The game leader turns on the radio so that there is music. As the music plays, players walk around the circle of chairs.

2. The leader can stop the music at any time. When she does, the players all have to sit on a chair. As there will be one less chair than players, two will have to share a chair.

3. With each round a chair is taken away. Players have to squeeze in more with each round so that all of the players can sit on the remaining chairs.

4. Chairs are taken away until players can no longer squeeze in on the chairs that remain. Then they count how many fit on the chairs and they start the game again.

78 Pin the Tail on the Donkey

A good sense of orientation and some luck are all that players need to put the tail on the donkey while blindfolded.

- **Age:** 5 years and up
- **Approximate Time:** 10 minutes
- **Players:** 5 or more
- **Materials:** a blindfold, cardboard, marker, a piece of rope, tape
- **Activity Level:** low

1. Draw an outline of a donkey without its tail on a piece of cardboard and hang it on the wall. Then, make the tail by unraveling the end of a rope, and place a piece of tape on it.

2. A player is chosen to be blindfolded. She is placed in front of the drawing of the donkey and spun around a few times.

3. The player then tries to pin the tail on the donkey in the correct place, following instructions that are given by her friends.

4. The player cannot touch the drawing before putting on the tail. When she decides where she has to go, she puts up her hand and pins it. The silly results will make all of the players watching laugh.

79 Upside-down World

In this game, the players' ability to react will help them do exactly the opposite of what they hear.

- **Age:** 5 years and up
- **Approximate Time:** 10 minutes
- **Players:** 6 or more
- **Materials:** none
- **Activity Level:** average

1. Players draw straws to choose a game leader. If the players are very young, an adult will be the game leader. The others form a circle around the leader.

2. The game leader gives different orders such as "One step forward" or "Hand on your head." All of the players do exactly the opposite, such as a step back or touch a foot.

3. The game leader gradually picks up the pace and complexity of the orders so that the players make mistakes. The game leader might also perform some of the actions as he says them to further confuse players.

4. The first player who makes a mistake or who is late in following the leader's instruction becomes the game leader, who then joins the others in the circle.

Mother Hen

A blindfold game in which the chicks have to find Mother Hen and take shelter under her wing. Everyone laughs in this game.

- **Age:** 6 years and up
- **Approximate Time:** 10 minutes
- **Players:** 6 or more
- **Materials:** a blindfold and piece of paper for each player
- **Activity Level:** average

1. Each player receives a folded piece of paper, one of which is marked with an X, which she looks at without showing to the others. The player who gets the paper with the X will be Mother Hen. The rest will be chicks.

2. Once the players know what their role is, they put on their blindfolds and start the game. Players walk around the room, feeling their way. When two players find each other, they whisper in each other's ear.

3. The chicks always say "cheep, cheep" and the Mother Hen says "cluck, cluck." When two chicks find each other, they say their two words and break apart. When a chick finds Mother Hen, he stays with her and holds onto her waist.

4. A chick cannot separate from Mother Hen once he has found her. The game continues until Mother Hen has all of her chicks at her side.

81 Poison Pencils

Balance is important in this game in which players have to carry a pencil without touching it or letting it fall to the ground.

- **Age:** 6 years and up
- **Approximate Time:** 10 minutes
- **Players:** 8 or more
- **Materials:** 2 pencils per player and 1 more per team
- **Activity Level:** low

1. Players form two or more teams with four players on each. Each player receives two pencils and holds one in each hand, taking it by the end. Teams form a circle.

2. One player on each team receives a third pencil, the "poison" pencil, and balances it on top of the other two so that she is holding it up without touching it with her hands.

3. When all of the teams are ready, a starting signal is given. The player who has the "poison" pencil passes it to the player on her right who will take it with his two pencils.

4. If the pencil falls, the team starts over. Players continue passing the pencil until it has gone one full circle without falling to the floor.

82 Night Guard

The "night guard" in this game depends on his hearing to protect his belongings from the "thieves."

- **Age:** 6 years and up
- **Approximate Time:** 10 minutes
- **Players:** 5 or more
- **Materials:** a blindfold, small objects, a newspaper
- **Activity Level:** low

1. Players draw straws to choose a night guard who will sit on the floor and put his belongings in front of him. These could be balloons, candy, and so on.

2. The guard then covers his eyes with the blindfold and holds a rolled-up newspaper in one hand. The other players crawl very stealthily toward him, trying to take one of his objects away.

3. If the guard hears anything, he can tap lightly in that direction with the newspaper. The player who is touched says his name and leaves the game.

4. When a player takes possession of one of the objects, he has to return to the starting point before he can try again. The game continues until there are no more objects or players left.

Blind Handkerchief

There is considerable noise in this game as players look for the handkerchief by following the instructions of their friends.

- **Age:** 6 years and up
- **Approximate Time:** 10 minutes
- **Players:** 9 or more
- **Materials:** a handkerchief, 2 blindfolds
- **Activity Level:** average

1. A game leader is chosen and the rest of the players form two teams. A line is drawn down the center of the playing area. The leader stands at one end of the line and the teams stand with their backs against one of the walls.

2. Each team receives a blindfold and players assign themselves numbers. When the game leader says a number, the player who has the number puts on the blindfold and crawls around trying to find the handkerchief.

3. The players of each team give instructions to their teammates, guiding them toward the handkerchief. When a player gets the handkerchief, he crawls back to his team.

4. The other player is eliminated from the game unless she catches the player with the handkerchief before he gets back to his team. In this case, the first player will be eliminated.

5. The game is played until one of the two teams is eliminated.

Lemon Race

The players on each team will pass a lemon as fast as they can, using only their chins to hold onto it.

- **Age:** 6 years and up
- **Approximate Time:** 5 minutes
- **Players:** 8 or more
- **Materials:** 1 lemon per team
- **Activity Level:** average

1. Players get into teams of four or more. The teams stand in a line and the first player in each line receives a lemon, which he holds by squeezing it between his chin and chest. He places his hands behind his back.

2. At the starting signal, the first player on each team turns around and tries to pass the lemon to the next player, who has to hold it in the same way.

3. Players cannot touch the lemon with their hands. If the lemon falls to the floor, it must be returned to the first player in line and the game starts over again.

4. The first team that is successful in passing the lemon to the last player without letting the lemon drop wins the game.

The Blacksmith

One of the players is the blacksmith and the others are his helpers. Players have to pay attention so they don't make a mistake with the gestures.

- **Age:** 7 years and up
- **Approximate Time:** 5 minutes
- **Players:** 6 or more
- **Materials:** none
- **Activity Level:** low

1. Players sit around a table and choose someone to be the blacksmith. All of the others will be his helpers and follow his instructions.

2. When the blacksmith says "Small nail" he hits the table with his pinky. When he says "Big nail" he does it with the palm of his hand. When he says "Very big nail" he does it with a closed fist. If it is "Gigantic nail" he does it with his foot.

3. The blacksmith hammers in different nails while he does the corresponding movements. The other players will imitate him without missing a beat.

4. When a player makes a mistake, he changes the hand he is playing with. If he makes another mistake, he is eliminated from the round. The helper who lasts the longest will be the blacksmith in the next round.

Point Basket

A game that provides a random mix of questions and tests. Players' actions are determined by the cards they choose.

- **Age:** 7 years and up
- **Approximate Time:** 30 minutes
- **Players:** 9 or more
- **Materials:** cardboard, scissors, marker, a tray
- **Activity Level:** average

1. Before starting the game, an adult prepares a series of cards. A question or a test, which players have to solve, is written on each card.

2. Questions can be on the order of "What is the biggest animal that lives in the sea?" or "What tree produces chestnuts?" The tests could be "Sing a song together for 30 seconds," or "Wrap the whole group in a streamer without breaking it."

3. After the cards have been prepared, they are put on a tray. Players form two groups and take turns picking a card from the tray. If the group answers a question correctly, it wins 1 point. If it performs a test well, it wins 3 points.

4. When a team gets a question wrong, the other can ask for a "rebound" and answer it. If that team gets the question right, it gets a point. If the team does not answer the question correctly, it loses a point. The first team to reach 10 points wins the game.

Chain of Spoons

A game testing players' skill at passing a marble to each other using spoons held in their mouths.

- **Age:** 7 years and up
- **Approximate Time:** 5 minutes
- **Players:** 6 or more
- **Materials:** 1 spoon per player, 1 marble per team
- **Activity Level:** low

1. Players form two teams with the same number of players on each. Each player receives a spoon and each team gets a marble. The groups stand in a circle.

2. Players hold the handle of the spoon in their mouths. The player with the marble puts

it on her spoon carefully so it doesn't fall off. At an agreed signal, she will try to pass the marble to the player on her right.

3. While the marble is being passed around, players cannot touch it with their hands. If the marble falls, the player who tried to pass it puts the marble back on his spoon.

4. The first team to successfully complete three rounds with the marble from spoon to spoon wins. If there are a lot of players on each time, fewer rounds can be played.

88 In the Bucket

All that is needed for this quiet game of aim that can be played inside the house are a wastepaper basket and an old deck of cards.

- **Age:** 8 years and up
- **Approximate Time:** 5 minutes
- **Players:** 2 or more
- **Materials:** a wastepaper basket, an old deck of cards
- **Activity Level:** low

1. Deal the cards out to the players and place the wastepaper basket about 7 feet from the shooting line. The basket should be empty and the cards old.

2. Players take turns tossing a card, trying to get it into the basket. To do this, players hold the card between their index finger and thumb and flick their wrist so that the card spins when it leaves the fingers.

3. Players earn 1 point for each basket they make. Face cards and aces count double.

4. A player can choose to "double," in which case the value of the card is doubled. However, if he misses the basket, he loses all of the points he has earned up to that point. When there are no more cards left, scores are tallied to see who the winner is.

89 Blowout!

This is a noisy and exciting game in which players blow up a balloon as fast as they can until it pops. DO NOT POP BALLOONS NEXT TO ANYBODY'S EAR!

- **Age:** 8 years and up
- **Approximate Time:** 5 minutes
- **Players:** 2 or more
- **Materials:** 1 balloon per player
- **Activity Level:** average

1. Each player receives a balloon to start the game. When all of the players have one, they stand in a circle and get ready to blow.

2. One of the players will give the signal to start by saying "One, two, three . . . go!" Then each player blows up his balloon as fast as he can until it explodes.

3. If a balloon gets away from a player, he picks it up and continues inflating it. The first player who pops his balloon wins.

4. The game continues until all of the balloons have popped. Players whose balloons have already burst cheer on their playmates until theirs also explode.

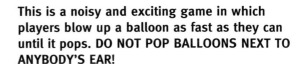

Flying Balloons

Players try to coordinate their movements in an effort to keep the maximum number of balloons in play and not let them touch the floor.

- **Age:** 8 years and up
- **Approximate Time:** 10 minutes
- **Players:** 6 or more
- **Materials:** 1 balloon per player
- **Activity Level:** average

1. Players divide up, forming two teams. The teams arrange themselves in two concentric circles so that one player is standing behind another.

2. Each player on the outside team blows up a balloon and knots it. When all of the balloons are blown up, the first player tosses her balloon into the inside circle.

3. Players in the inside circle keep the balloon up by touching it with any part of their body, but they cannot hold the balloons. Players in the outside circle will count five touches and then toss another balloon.

4. Every time players on the inside touch a balloon five times, the outside team will toss another one for them to keep in motion. When a balloon touches the floor, players see how many balloons they had and change roles.

Games

1oo

for the Snow

A snowy landscape provides one of the most complete and fun play settings that one can imagine, both for the possibilities it offers and because it happens during only one season of the year and only in certain parts of the world. To make the most of this opportunity, we present here a selection of games that can be enjoyed in the snow.

10 games for the snow, both old and new, in which children shape it, roll around in it, and use it to have fun practicing aim, skill, and speed. One should always be well equipped when playing in snow.

91 Columns

A game of aim in which the snow is shaped to form all of the elements necessary to play.

- **Age:** 6 years and up
- **Approximate Time:** 5 minutes
- **Players:** 2 or more
- **Materials:** snow
- **Activity Level:** average

1. Each player makes three small columns about 6 inches high, packing the snow with their hands. All of the columns have to be in the same line.

2. After the columns have been made, players take five steps back and establish an order for tossing. The throwing distance can vary, depending on the age of the players.

3. Players take turns making a snowball and throwing it at the columns, trying to hit one of them. If a player succeeds, she gets a point.

4. Players continue the game until there are no more columns left standing. The player who knocks over the most columns wins. Then all of the players help shape new columns to play again.

92 White

A game of visual perception in which all of the players try to find small white objects in the snow.

- **Age:** 6 years and up
- **Approximate Time:** 10 minutes
- **Players:** 2 or more
- **Materials:** 3 small white objects per person
- **Activity Level:** average

1. Each player holds in her hands three small white objects, such as Ping-Pong balls, plastic caps, or pieces of chalk.

2. All of the players stand on a line with their backs turned and count aloud "One, two, three!" When they get to "three,"

players toss their objects backward over their head as far as they can.

3. After they throw their objects, players count to three again and go to look for the objects in the snow. Players have to have sharp eyes because the objects get lost in the snow.

4. After all of the objects have been found, players count up how many they picked up to see who has the best vision. When the game is over, the objects are removed from the snow.

Basket of Snow

A game of aim in which players not only have to get the ball in the basket, but they have to do so without hitting an obstacle.

- **Age:** 6 years and up
- **Approximate Time:** 10 minutes
- **Players:** 2 or more
- **Materials:** snow
- **Activity Level:** average

1. Make a "basket" about 1 foot wide and 6 inches high out of snow. Use well-packed snow to shape an arc to make a handle for the top of the basket.

2. After the basket has been made, players stand 5 feet back from it and make snowballs that they will take turns tossing into it.

3. If a player gets the first ball in, he earns 1 point and can throw a second snowball, which will be worth 2 points, and so on.

4. A player does not get all of the points he has accumulated in the round until he misses a throw or leaves the game. If a throw touches the handle over the basket, the player loses all of the points he has won in the round and the turn passes to the next player.

94 Sledding

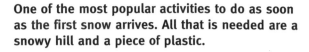

One of the most popular activities to do as soon as the first snow arrives. All that is needed are a snowy hill and a piece of plastic.

- **Age:** 6 years and up
- **Approximate Time:** 30 minutes
- **Players:** 2 or more
- **Materials:** sleds or heavy plastic
- **Activity Level:** high

1. A snowy hill that is not too steep and that does not have any obstacle such as trees or rocks is all that is needed for sledding.

2. Before taking off down the slope, the hill should be checked out on foot to be sure it does not contain any obstacles and that the ground is smooth. After this is done, players climb to the top of the hill with their sleds.

3. Children can use bought or homemade sleds to slide down the hill. Or they can simply use a heavy piece of plastic.

4. If plastic is used, players sit on it, either singly, in pairs, or in threes, and slide on the snow, guiding the improvised sled with their heels.

95 Eskimo Circle

A game originated by the Eskimos who, because of the climate they live in, have made snow a wonderful place to play.

- **Age:** 6 years and up
- **Approximate Time:** 5 minutes
- **Players:** 5 or more
- **Materials:** snow
- **Activity Level:** low

1. All of the players form a circle, standing as close to each other as they can and extending their bare hands with the palms upward in front of them.

2. After the circle of palms has been formed, with each one touching the other, one of the players makes a small snowball, puts it in his hand, and returns his hand to the circle.

3. The player who has the snowball tilts her hand a little so that the snowball rolls onto the hand to her left. That player repeats the movement so that the snowball goes around the circle.

4. The movement accelerates so that the ball goes around the circle until it falls on the ground or melts from the warmth of the hands.

Long Jump

In this game, the snow helps to cushion a player's fall and mark the distance he jumped.

- **Age:** 6 years and up
- **Approximate Time:** 10 minutes
- **Players:** 2 or more
- **Materials:** snow
- **Activity Level:** high

1. Players look for a smooth ground that is covered with a uniform layer of snow. They mark two parallel lines about 30 feet apart.

2. They then stomp the ground between the two lines to smooth it out and pile up a little more snow behind the second line.

3. Players take turns running toward the second line and from there jumping forward as far as possible. Their heel prints will mark their distance.

4. After each jump, footprints are checked to see if the player jumped in front of or behind the line. If the jump is valid, the heel marks are left in the snow and the next player jumps.

Follow Yeti

A very amusing game of hide-and-seek suitable for playing in a wooded area where players can easily hide.

- **Age:** 7 years and up
- **Approximate Time:** 30 minutes
- **Players:** 2 or more
- **Materials:** snow
- **Activity Level:** average

1. A large expanse of snow-covered ground where footprints can be left is needed for this game. After finding a place like this, players draw straws to see who Yeti will be.

2. Yeti leaves the group and walks in a heavy way to leave footprints. The other players stay in one place without looking and wait for 5 minutes.

3. After the agreed time has passed, players set out to look for Yeti, following his footprints. Yeti will try to throw them off his trail by walking backward over his own footprints or by hopping on one foot, for example.

4. If Yeti returns to the starting point without being seen, he is saved. Otherwise, the first player who finds him will be the next Yeti.

98 Rescue

A quiet game that combines luck and skill in picking up three rings buried in the snow.

- **Age:** 7 years and up
- **Approximate Time:** 10 minutes
- **Players:** 2 or more
- **Materials:** 3 rings 2 inches in diameter, a twig, or a wire
- **Activity Level:** low

1. Prepare three rings and a stick with a hook on the end. For rings, you can use the plastic pieces from a roll of tape, and a piece of wire can be used to make the hook.

2. One player will make a square in the snow about two hands wide and then divide it into smaller squares. She will then bury each ring in any of three squares. The other players should not see where she buries the rings.

3. Players take turns poking the hook in the snow trying to fish out the buried rings.

4. If there are only two players, they tally up the tries it took them to find the rings and then they change roles. If there are more than two players, each one counts the rings she has found.

99 Snow Mound

A throwing game in which precision is very important to calculate how far the snowball will roll.

- **Age:** 8 years and up
- **Approximate Time:** 10 minutes
- **Players:** 2 or more
- **Materials:** snow
- **Activity Level:** average

1. Smooth out a rectangular area of snow about 30 feet long by 3 feet wide. Shape a mound at one end of the rectangle about 1 foot from the back line.

2. Players stand at the opposite end of the rectangle and make three snowballs each. Then they establish an order of play.

3. Players take turns rolling their snowball down the rectangular area, trying to get it as close as possible to the mound.

4. If a snowball breaks apart on its roll, or if it rolls into another snowball, it doesn't count. The player who gets the most balls to touch the mound wins.

Snake Slide

A game played by various Native American groups during the winter months. It is played over a frozen surface.

- **Age:** 8 years and up
- **Approximate Time:** 5 minutes
- **Players:** 2 or more
- **Materials:** 1 branch per player
- **Activity Level:** average

1. Players must find a long frozen surface. This game was originally played on a frozen river or lake. If players do this, they have to be absolutely sure that the surface is totally frozen before stepping onto it.

2. Each player tries to find a straight branch about 6 inches long that will be his "snake." Look around on the ground for a branch before cutting one from a tree.

3. Players stand at a predetermined spot and take turns throwing their "snake" so that it slides as far as possible over the icy surface.

4. After all of the branches have been tossed, players look to see which one slid the farthest and who the winner is. The game is played again.

Alphabetical Index

Name of the Game	Page	Age (from)	Approximate Time	Players	Materials	Activity
"ABC"	52	7	10 min.	7 or more	yes	average
Achi	27	6	5 min.	2	yes	low
Animal, Vegetable, or Mineral?	15	8	5 min.	2 or more	no	low
Ati Dada	36	7	5 min.	2	yes	low
Awelé	40	8	30 min.	2	yes	low
Badum	12	7	5 min.	2 or more	no	low
Basket of Snow	73	6	10 min.	2 or more	yes	average
Blacksmith (The)	66	7	5 min.	6 or more	no	low
Blind Handkerchief	65	6	10 min.	9 or more	yes	average
Blowout!	68	8	5 min.	2 or more	yes	average
Buzz	18	10	5 min.	5 or more	no	low
Chain of Spoons	67	7	5 min.	6 or more	yes	low
Chicago	44	9	10 min.	2 or more	yes	low
Circle (The)	48	3	5 min.	3 or more	yes	average
Circle of Bubbles	59	4	10 min.	8 or more	yes	average
Circle Soccer	51	7	10 min.	12 or more	yes	average
Colorful Hands	58	4	5 min.	5 or more	no	low
Columns	72	6	5 min.	2 or more	yes	average
Crowned!	44	10	30 min.	2 or more	yes	low
Dead!	30	7	5 min.	2 or more	yes	low
Detective (The)	19	10	30 min.	10 or more	yes	low
Dominoes	29	6	10 min.	2 or more	yes	low
Donkey	32	7	5 min.	3 or more	yes	low
Draw Two	38	8	10 min.	2 or more	yes	low
Eight Stacks	28	6	5 min.	2	yes	low
Eskimo Circle	74	6	5 min.	5 or more	yes	low
Farm (The)	26	6	10 min.	3 or more	yes	low
Five Paths (The)	33	7	5 min.	2	yes	low
Five!	40	8	10 min.	2 or more	yes	low
Flying Ball	54	8	30 min.	8 or more	yes	high
Flying Balloons	69	8	10 min.	6 or more	yes	average
Follow Yeti	75	7	30 min.	2 or more	yes	average
Forbidden Letter	17	9	5 min.	2 or more	no	low
Four Alike	36	7	10 min.	2	yes	low
Friendly Handkerchief	53	8	30 min.	11 or more	yes	high
Go	43	9	30 min.	2	yes	low
Go-moku	27	6	5 min.	2	yes	low
Hands and Feet	16	8	5 min.	6 or more	no	average
Headlines	22	11	30 min.	4 or more	yes	low
How Many?	11	6	5 min.	2 or more	yes	low
Hus (The)	42	9	30 min.	2	yes	low
Hyena in Pursuit	30	6	5 min.	2 or more	yes	low
"I'm Going to . . ."	20	10	5 min.	5 or more	no	low
Initials	14	8	10 min.	4 or more	no	low
In the Bucket	68	8	5 min.	2 or more	yes	low
Jump Rope Race	52	8	5 min.	2 or more	yes	high
King (The)	45	10	30 min.	3 or more	yes	low
Kiriki	41	9	10 min.	2 or more	yes	low

Name of the Game	Page	Age (from)	Approximate Time	Players	Materials	Activity
Knock Down the Pin	55	10	30 min.	10 or more	yes	average
Lemon Race	66	6	5 min.	8 or more	yes	average
Lightbulb (The)	51	6	10 min.	5 or more	yes	average
Long Jump	75	6	10 min.	2 or more	yes	high
Mother Hen	63	6	10 min.	6 or more	yes	average
Musical Chairs	61	5	10 min.	6 or more	yes	average
Mystery Person (The)	21	10	10 min.	6 or more	no	low
Mystery Taste	60	5	10 min.	5 or more	yes	low
Night Guard	64	6	10 min.	5 or more	yes	low
Old Maid	26	6	10 min.	2 or more	yes	low
Passes Between Bases	55	9	30 min.	10 or more	yes	average
Pile (The)	17	9	5 min.	5 or more	no	low
Pin the Tail on the Donkey	62	5	10 min.	5 or more	yes	low
Point Basket	67	7	30 min.	9 or more	yes	average
Poison Pencils	64	6	10 min.	8 or more	yes	low
Prisoners	49	5	10 min.	8 or more	no	average
Puluc	32	7	10 min.	2	yes	low
Rescue	76	7	10 min.	2 or more	yes	low
Ring (The)	48	3	5 min.	6 or more	no	average
Scrambled Syllables	15	8	5 min.	3 or more	no	low
Seega	39	8	10 min.	2	yes	low
Series (The)	35	7	10 min.	2 or more	yes	low
Serious Circle	8	4	5 min.	5 or more	no	low
Shepherd's Goat (The)	54	9	10 min.	10 or more	yes	average
Simon Says	9	5	5 min.	3 or more	no	low
Sledding	74	6	30 min.	2 or more	yes	high
Snake Slide	77	8	5 min.	2 or more	yes	average
Snow Mound	76	8	10 min.	2 or more	yes	average
Solitaire	38	8	30 min.	1	yes	low
Stepping on Balloons	61	5	5 min.	5 or more	yes	high
Storytellers (The)	12	7	10 min.	2 or more	yes	low
Switch Teams	50	6	10 min.	6 or more	yes	average
Tablut	37	8	30 min.	2	yes	low
Tap, Tap	23	11	10 min.	7 or more	no	low
There Are Four	8	5	5 min.	2 or more	no	low
Thirty-six	41	8	5 min.	2 or more	yes	low
This Way	14	8	10 min.	3 or more	no	low
Three Errors	22	11	30 min.	5 or more	no	low
Three Investigators (The)	20	10	10 min.	8 or more	yes	low
Time to Get Dressed!	60	4	10 min.	8 or more	yes	average
Treasure Hunt	58	4	10 min.	6 or more	yes	average
Trios	50	5	10 min.	6 or more	no	high
True or False?	18	10	10 min.	3 or more	no	low
Tunnel (The)	49	5	5 min.	8 or more	no	average
Turkish Checkers	35	7	10 min.	2	yes	low
Upside-down World	62	5	10 min.	6 or more	no	average
White	72	6	10 min.	2 or more	yes	average
Who Are You?	10	6	10 min.	3 or more	no	low
Who's Who?	13	7	10 min.	10 or more	no	low
XO	31	7	5 min.	2	yes	low
Zamma	34	7	10 min.	2	yes	low
Zip, Zap, Zup	21	11	5 min.	6 or more	no	low

Bibliography

Bartl, Almuth. *Eddie's Finger Quiz Books* (six in the series). Hauppauge, NY: Barron's Educational Series, Inc., 2000.

Belka, David. *Teaching Children Games: Becoming a Master Teacher.* Champaign, IL: Human Kinetics Publications, 1994.

Childre, Doc Lew, et al. *Teaching Children to Love: 80 Games & Fun Activities for Raising Balanced Children in Unbalanced Times.* Boulder Creek, CA: Planetary Publications, 1996.

Collis, Len. *Card Games for Children.* Hauppauge, NY: Barron's Educational Series, Inc., 1989.

Feldman, Jean R. *The Complete Handbook of Indoor and Outdoor Games and Activities for Young Children.* Upper Saddle River, NJ: Prentice Hall, 1994.

Kirchner, Glenn. *Children's Games from Around the World.* Needham Heights, MA: Allyn & Bacon, 2000.

Perez, Eulalia. *100 Best Games.* Hauppauge, NY: Barron's Educational Series, Inc., 2000.

Powell, Dorothy et al. Juba This and Juba That: *100 African-American Games for Children.* New York: Simon and Schuster, 1996.

Roopnarine, Jaipaul (ed.), et al. *Children's Play in Diverse Cultures.* New York: State University of New York, 1994.

Stott, Dorothy M. *The Big Book of Games.* New York: Dutton Books, 1998.

Swan, Ann. *How to Make Games for Children: A Handbook of Noncompetitive Games Written for Parents & Educators for Use with Children Ages 2 Thru 12.* Woodinville, WA: Pound Publishing, 1986.

Acknowledgments

To Maqui, for everything; to my parents, who never tired of playing with us; to ATZAR, Associació de Ludoteques de Catalunya (Association of Game Libraries of Catalonia); to the Ludoteca La Guineu (La Guineu Game Library); to Kidege; to SOS Racisme; to the Club de Go la Pedra (la Pedra Go Club); to the Federació Catalana de Dominó per Parelles (Catalan Federation of Dominoes Partners); and to IOCARE, Coordinadora de Entidades de Juego (Coordinator of Gaming Entities).